The Book Belongs To.

Be kind
TO YOUR
Mind

It's Ok
Not To
Be Ok

Mental
Health
Matters

Make Yourself A Priority

Believe
IN
yourself

fight
HOPE
LOVE

Mental Health

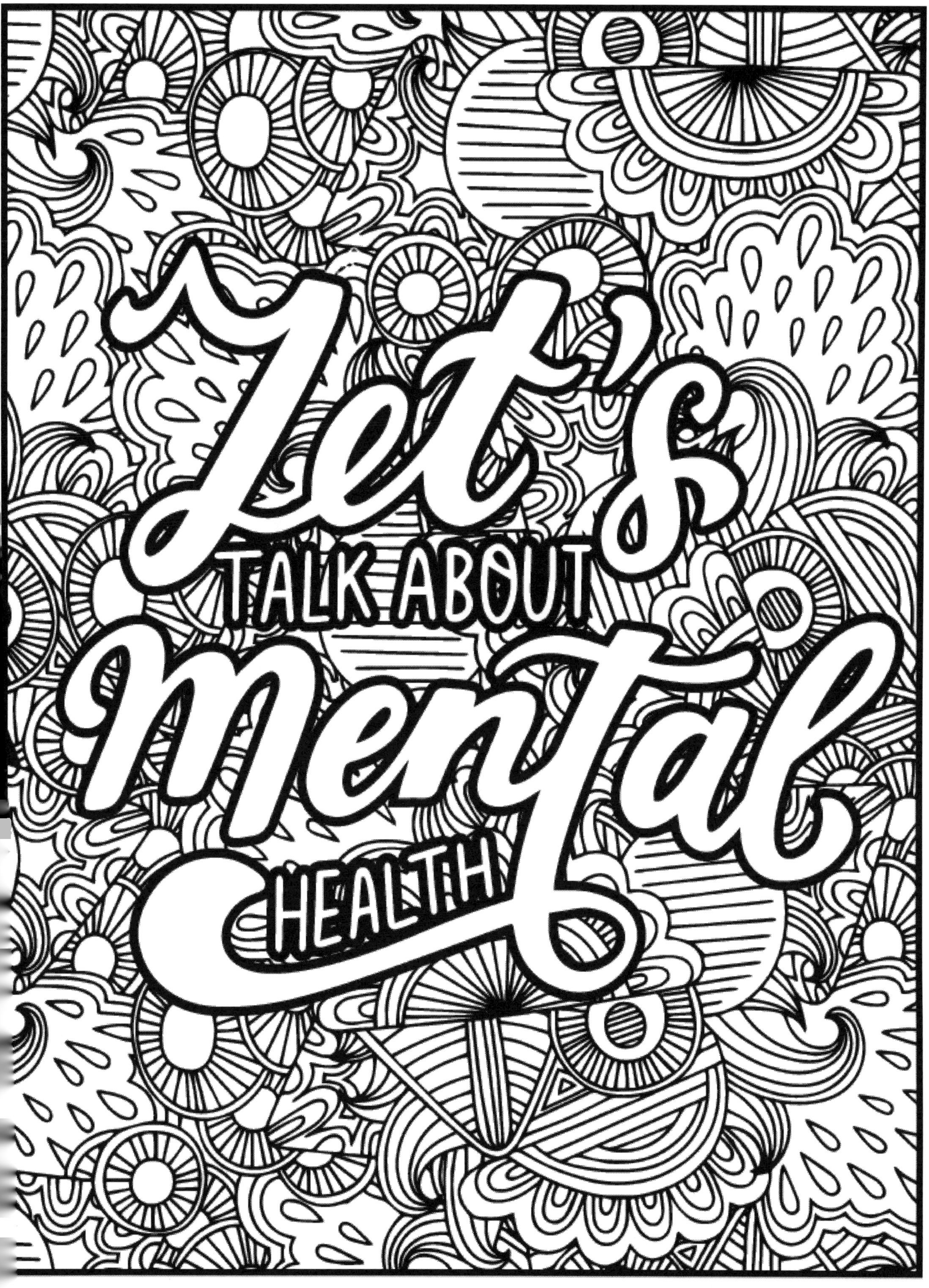
Let's
TALK ABOUT
Mental
HEALTH

hard
TIMES
do not
LAST FOREVER

Be safe

STOP
DOUBTING
YOURSELF

You've
Totally
Got This

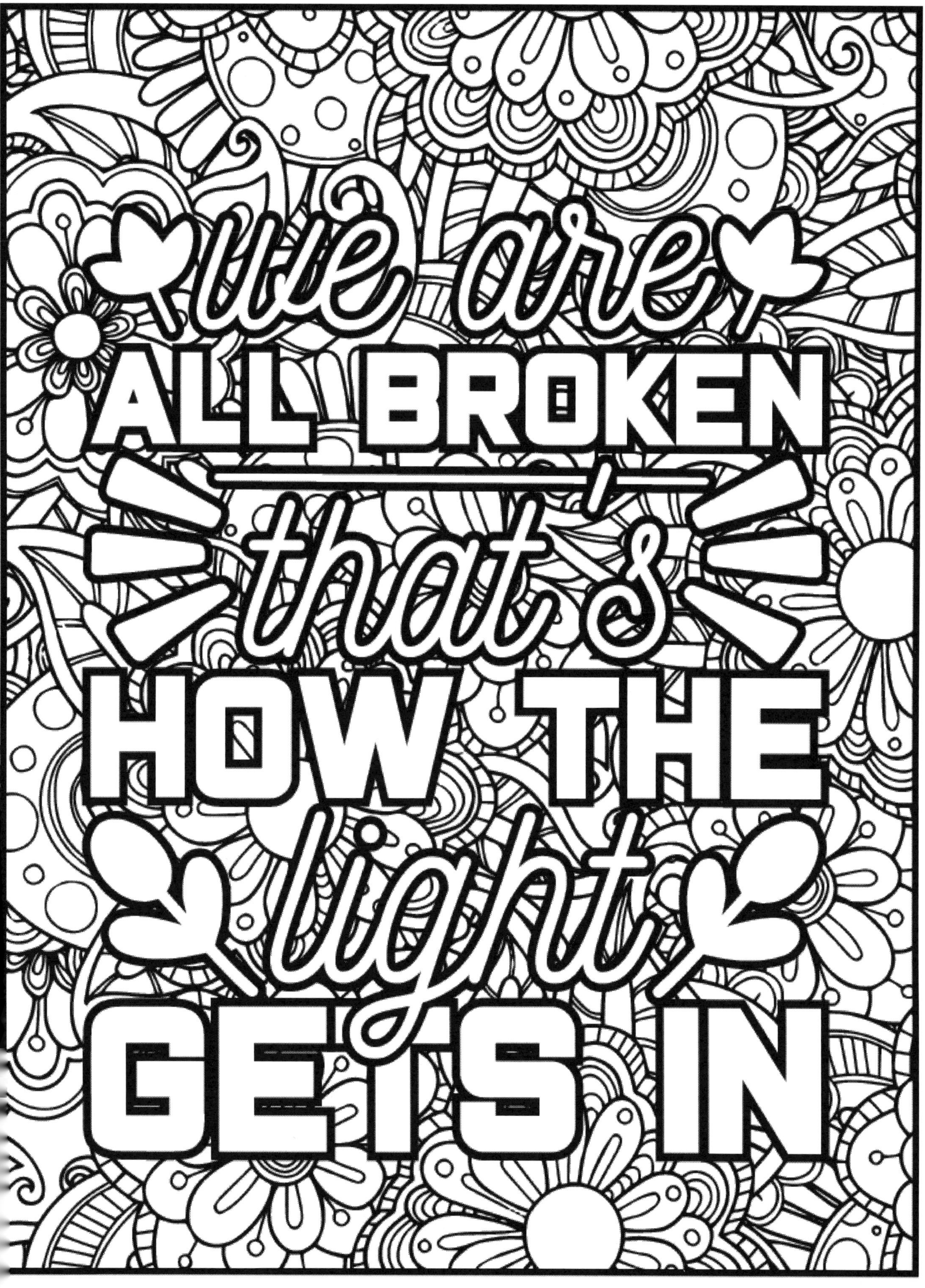
we are
ALL BROKEN
that's
HOW THE
light
GETS IN

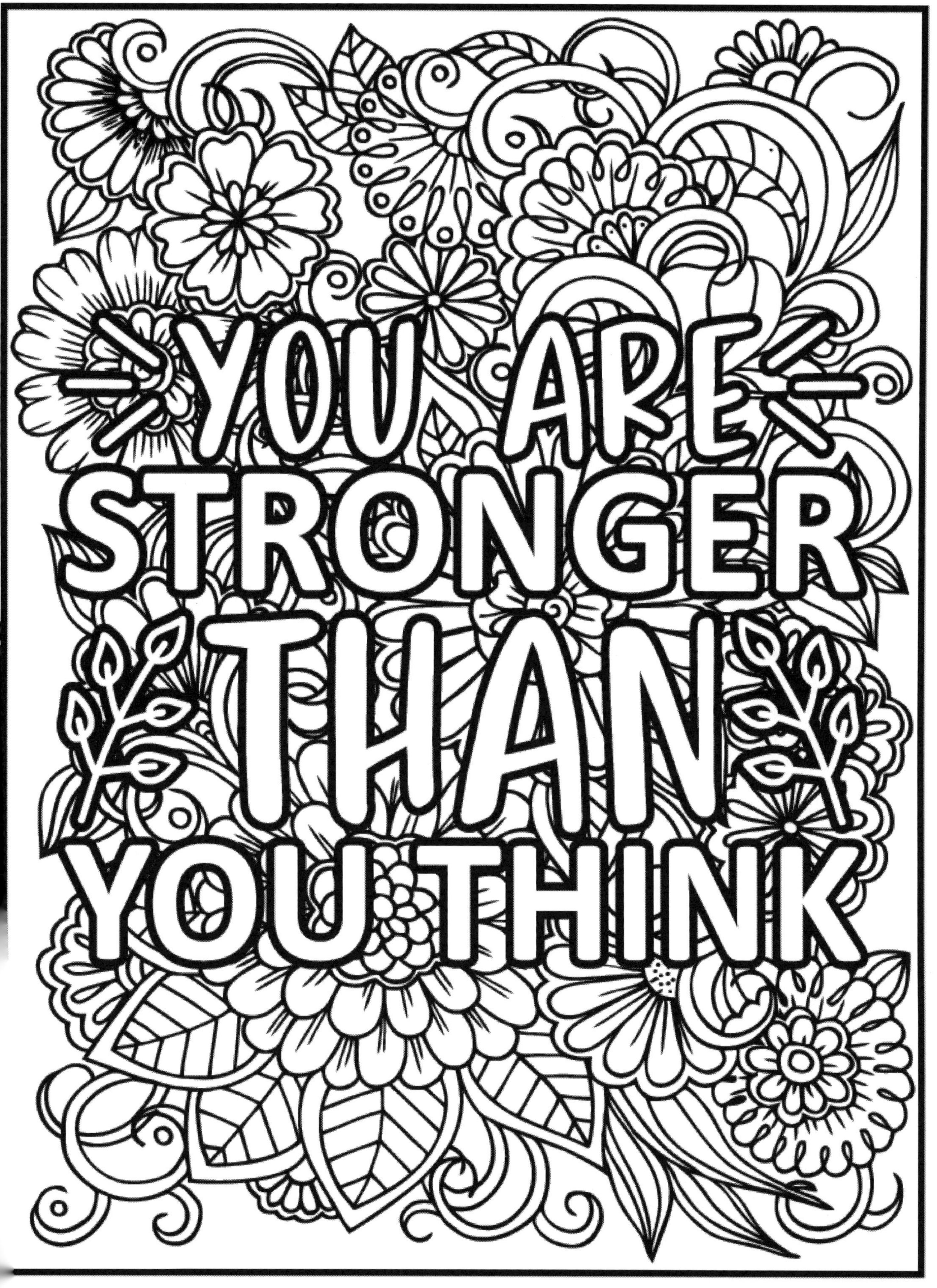
YOU ARE
STRONGER
THAN
YOU THINK

Don't Be
So Hard
On Yourself

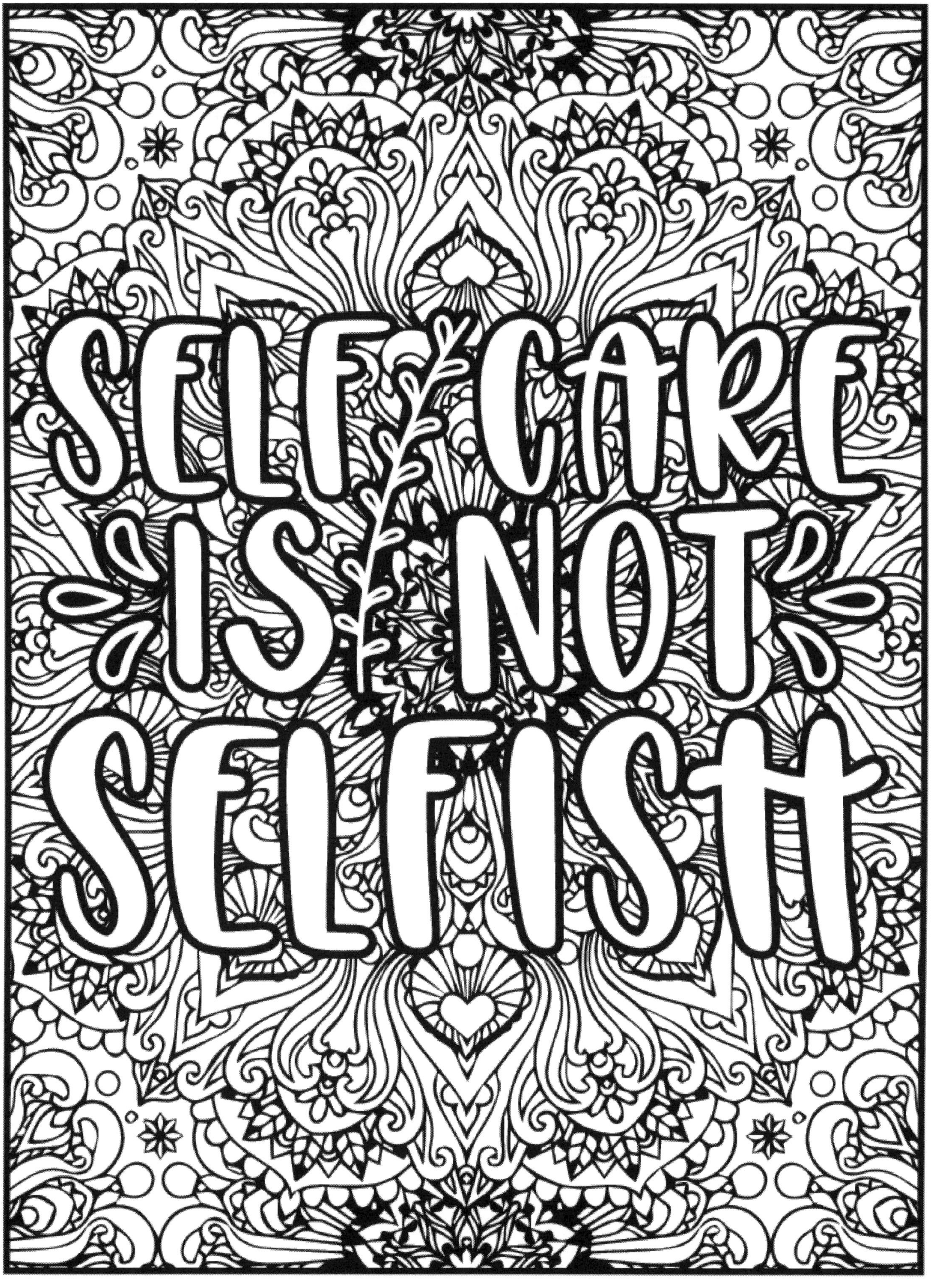
SELF CARE
IS NOT
SELFISH

my story
is not
over

YOU
are
ENOUGH

You Matter

STARS
can't
SHINE
without
DARKNESS

REMEMBER
THAT
YOU ARE
AMAZING

YOUR FEAR
is lying
TO YOU

life is
TOUGH
but so
ARE YOU

TOMORROW
needs
YOU

HOLD ON
Pain
ENDS

Let's
SELF
CARE

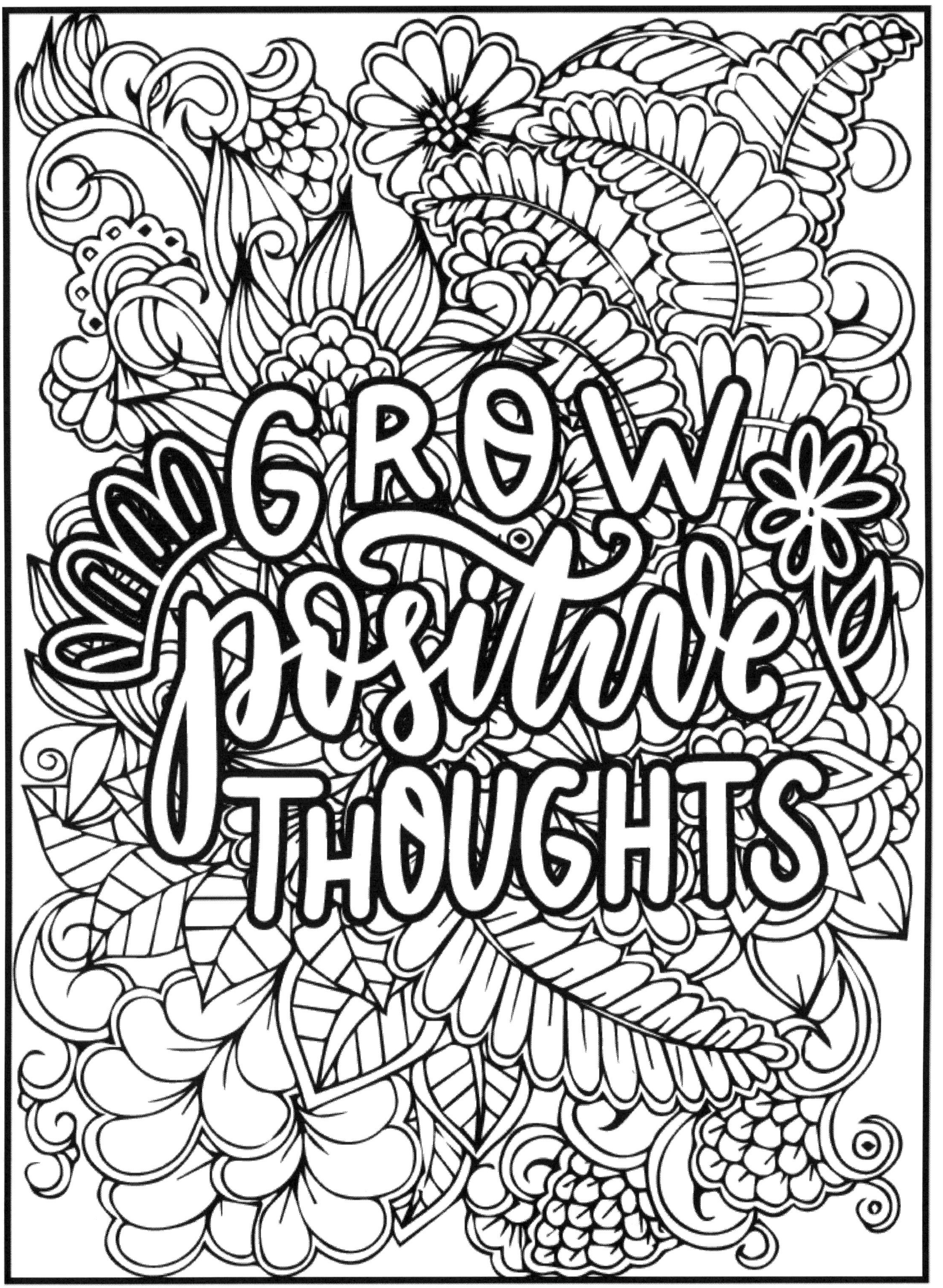
GROW
positive
THOUGHTS

LISTEN
TO YOUR
HEART

Stop
breathe
Be!

SHE
believed
SHE COULD
SO
she DID

Made in the USA
Monee, IL
03 November 2024

69205594R00035